World Atavism

Nadakkavu, Kozhikode, Kerala, 673011
www.insightpublica.com
e-mail: insightpublica@gmail.com

Title: **World Atavism**
Author: **Edmond Hamilton**
First Insight Edition: August 2024
Copyright © Reserved
All rights reserved.
Printed and Published by
InsightinPublica Printers & Publishers Pvt. Ltd.
ISBN: 978-93-5517-520-5

World Atavism

Edmond Hamilton

INSIGHT PUBLICA ®

Edmond Hamilton

(21 October 1904 - 1 February 1977)

Edmond Moore Hamilton was an American writer
of science fiction during the mid-twentieth century.

FOREWORD

I write these words in a room perched high in one of New York's highest towers. Beneath me, in the fading sunlight of late afternoon, there stretches the vast mass of the mighty city's structures. New York it is—but such a New York as never man looked upon before. And it is with its familiar but infinitely strange panorama before my eyes that I start now this record of the great change.

****

My name is Allan Harker. Dr. Allan Harker, I could say, for it has been seven years since I took the degree and with it a position on the biological staff of Manhattan University. That was a great day for me. Manhattan was one of the most renowned of eastern universities, and its biological department in particular was known to scientists the world over. This was due not only to the department's unrivalled equipment, but also in greater part to two of the scientists who worked in it, Dr. Howard Grant, head of the department, and Dr. Raymond Ferson, his associate. Very proud I was to have won so soon the opportunity of working with those two world-famed biologists. And even prouder I was when, in the next years, my work came gradually to link my name with theirs.

Grant and Ferson and Harker—we were known to scientists across half the world. It was Grant, of course, the eldest of us, who was best known. A tall, saturnine-faced and dark-browed Scotsman, his utter and undivided passion for research was a byword among us. It used to be said, though not in his hearing, that Grant would have vivisected his own grandmother if he thought some new principle might be learned by it. All respected the man, or the man's achievements, but he never had a tithe of the popularity that was Ferson's. Ferson was in fact a complete contrast to his superior, a short-statured man of middle age with unruly hair and beard and warm brown, friendly eyes. As for myself, the third of the trio, I had neither the brilliant scientific mind of Grant nor the keen vision of Ferson, but by dint of ceaseless plodding with monotonous details, I had built for myself a reputation that linked my name with theirs.

Aside from our professorial duties in the university's lecture-rooms, we had each of us our separate work. I was plodding away with my dull experiments on cell-grouping, which I expected would some day yield a theory that would astound all cytologists. Now and then I received help on some difficult point from Ferson, who was himself immersed in an attempt to demolish the Snelsen-Morrs re-vertebration theory by prying into the interior structure of innumerable unheard-of lizards. Grant, however, never received or gave any help, keeping his work entirely to himself. We had gathered, from his rare references to it, that he had been working for months on one of the broader problems of evolutionary science, but that was all we knew, and we were as amazed as any when Grant published the statement that touched off the sensational "evolution controversy."

It is needless for me to give here all the details of the thing. It is sufficient to say that Grant, in his statement, announced that he had solved at last the greatest enigma of biological science—that he had discovered the cause of evolution.

One can understand what an uproar that statement created, and was bound to create. For the cause of evolutionary change has always been the supreme problem of biology. Long ago Darwin and Wallace and Lamarck and their fellows had laid the processes of evolution bare. They had shown to an astonished world that life on earth was not static in forms that had always existed and always would exist, but that it was in constant change and movement up through constantly changing forms. The eohippus had changed, had evolved into the horse, and in future ages would be something different still. The great felines that had roamed earth had evolved into smaller forms and into tame cats. A certain branch of ape-like forms had evolved into great hairy troglodytes and then into modern men. All life on earth was constantly changing, evolving, forced ever upward through the diverging channels of evolution into new and different forms.

But what force was it that pressed earth's life thus upward through the paths of change? What force was it that caused all this vast, slow evolution of earth's creatures into different creatures, that had begun with the first jelly-like life-forms on earth and had forced the tide of life up from them to the forms of today, that still was slowly changing them? That question none could answer. Environment did not explain it, for though environment had certain effects on the life-forms in it, it was not responsible for that deep, vast tide of upward evolution. Mendelism had seemed for a time to suggest an explanation but had failed in the end to do so. Some great force there was, all knew, that pressed life always up the path of evolution, but none had ever guessed what that force might be, and the thing had come to be accepted at last as one of the insoluble problems of science. And now Grant claimed that he had solved it!

"For long," Grant's statement said, "I have held that since evolutionary change is unquestionably caused by some definite and omnipresent force acting upon all life on earth, it should be possible to discover the nature of that force. I will not recount the work of months which I have spent in constant search for this force, but will say that finally I have been successful, have identified the force which my experiments show beyond all doubt to be the single force responsible for the upward course of evolution on earth. That force is a vibratory force, a vibration unknown to earth's physicists prior to my discovery of it, which has as its source the sun!

"The sun, we know, is a vast mass of incandescent matter which ceaselessly pours out part of its matter transformed into energy. The energy thus formed, flooding out in all directions from the sun through space, takes various forms. At a certain vibratory frequency, it takes the form of light and illuminates our day. At another frequency, it is radiant heat, warming our world. At still another, it is the cosmic ray so recently discovered. There are many others, known to us, and still more of which we know nothing as yet, a vast welter of vibratory forces flooding endlessly outward from the sun. And it is one of those vibrations, one which we well may call the evolution vibration, which is responsible for the evolutionary change of all life on earth.

"In this there is nothing astounding. The sun's various vibratory forces affect all living things on earth profoundly, each in a different manner. Without the light-vibrations earth's life would fade and die, the absence of the ultra-violet waves being fatal in time. Without its heat-radiations all life would freeze. And without this evolution vibration playing ceaselessly upon earth, all life upon earth would no longer be pressed upward through the paths of evolution, would slip back swiftly down those paths, down the myriad roads up which it has surged for so long. For not only is it this evolution vibration that forces earth's life upward on the way of change, it is this vibration that keeps earth's life from slipping backward!"

Thus for Grant's statement. To Ferson and me it was as astonishing as to the rest of the scientific world, for not until then did we learn what work it was that had occupied Grant for so long. Yet even we two, I think, were surprised at the sensation that that statement caused. Always the work of Dr. Grant had been accepted almost without question, so great was his reputation and so brilliant his achievements. But with the publication of this amazing new theory of his, the general dislike of the man that had always lain latent, burst forth into a storm of criticism.

It was admitted that the new vibratory force which Grant had discovered did apparently exist, since other scientists working on his data had corroborated his work on it. But it was denied, by Grant's numerous critics, that this force was what he claimed it to be—the cause of evolutionary change. It was impossible, they stated, that such a so-called evolution vibration could in reality be responsible for the course of evolution on earth. And it was even more absurd to suggest as Grant had done that were that force withdrawn, were the evolution vibration to cease to play on earth from the sun, the living beings of earth would slip swiftly backward on the road of change.

The controversy over the thing grew, in fact, to a point of bitterness unprecedented in scientific discussion, a bitterness intensified by the comments of the saturnine and black-tempered Grant. In a series of sardonic statements, he compared his critics to those who had derided the work of Darwin and his fellows, and indulged in some rather acrid personalities. These in turn provoked fiercer attacks, and the whole matter grew thus quickly into an unseemly intellectual brawl. To Ferson and myself the whole controversy seemed a useless one, because, in the course of time, experimentation by other scientists would definitely prove or disprove Grant's theory. Yet neither of us ventured to suggest that to our bitter superior, and so the wrangle grew in intensity in the next days until it suddenly came to a head.

It was the elderly President Rogers of Manhattan University who brought the thing to a focus. He and the university's other officials had been growing more and more restive under the criticisms that Grant's controversy was bringing on the school, and so at last he suggested that a meeting be held at which Grant could lay his theories and data before his fellow-scientists in their entirety. This Grant accepted, and so too did most biologists of any note within traveling distance of New York, so widely had the clamor of the dispute spread. And on an afternoon Grant rose before several hundred assembled scientists in one of the university's lecture-halls to explain his discovery.

There is little need for me to tell at length of what took

place at that meeting, which both Ferson and I attended. At the first appearance of Dr. Grant his enemies in the audience grew vocal in their criticisms, and before he had spoken a quarter of an hour the hall was in such an uproar as a scientific meeting has seldom heard. Twice Grant made an effort to go on and each time his voice was drowned by a storm of shouted cries. The President, chairman of the meeting, was rapping vainly for order, but Grant only stood still, looking out over the stormy meeting with a cold contempt in his eyes, yet with a strange fire in them. Quietly he rolled up the data-sheets in his hand and thrust them into his pocket, and as quietly stepped forward to the platform's edge. Something in his bearing, in his expression, quickly quieted the noisy throng before him.

His voice came out over the hall cold and clear. "You have not let me give to you the proof for which you asked," he said.

The President stepped to his side, said something rapidly, but Grant shook his head calmly. "No proof that I can give you here would convince you of my theory's truth, I know," he told the silent throng before him, "but I will give you proof of it yet! To you, and to the world, I will give a proof such as the world has never seen before!"

Before any could move, he had walked from the platform and out of the hall. A buzz of excited voices broke out instantly, in comment and criticism. It was some hours later before Ferson and I got from the meeting to Grant's laboratory. But Grant was not there.

Within twenty-four hours more we knew, and all at

the university knew, that Dr. Grant had disappeared. From the meeting he went to his laboratory, burned some papers there and pocketed others. Then he went to his rooms, hastily packed a few bags and departed. He left no note, no message. His action brought to a climax the whole sensation of the controversy he had precipitated and Grant's going was taken by many of his critics as a confession of the falsity of his position. He had had no close relatives to start a search for him, and though to Ferson and me his strange departure seemed astounding, we could explain it no better than others. The sensation subsided, and Ferson was appointed to head the department in place of the vanished scientist. Our own work occupied us once more. And certainly neither Ferson nor I, any more than another, guessed what lay behind Grant's strange action.

****

It was six months after Grant's departure that the great change began.

The first intimation was brought to the public notice by a New York newspaper. In a sensational article entitled "Is a New Crime Wave Upon Us?" it pointed out that in the last few days an unprecedented number of crimes of violence had taken place.

These were the more appalling in that many seemed quite without motive. In New York alone, in those few days, there had been more than a dozen murders, mostly clubbings and stabbings, which had apparently been provoked by the slightest of causes. In Chicago a respected clerk of middle age had for some annoyance turned suddenly and fractured the skulls of three of his associates with a heavy bar. From San Francisco and Los Angeles had come news of half a dozen holocausts in which one member of a family had slaughtered or attempted to slaughter all the others. From every part of the land there were coming reports of the most horrifying crimes of violence, the great majority of which seemed inspired by the pettiest of causes.

And this same wave of homicidal mania seemed at work over all the world! It was as though hundreds in earth's population had suddenly had their reason dwarfed and their passions magnified. No less than three solid householders in London had run amuck in bursts of sadistic[1] fury that had cost a half-score lives. The Paris police had taken from the Seine more human bodies, many terribly mutilated, than had ever been found in it in a like time before. Germany was aghast over two mass-murders of unexampled fiendishness that had occurred in a Rhenish and a Silesian village. There was news of an even more terrible slaying in Calcutta, and word of murders almost as terrible from almost every country on the globe.

Nor was it murder alone that was stalking the earth, for robberies of the utmost brutality were even more numerous. Overshadowed as they were by the greater horror, they were as astonishing in nature. For all, like the slayings, seemed the result of sudden brutal instincts or desires uncontrolled by reason. Small shopkeepers in American and English towns were struck down for trifles. In the stores of great cities there were those who snatched childishly at desired objects and attempted a hopeless escape to the street. That was the keynote of all these robberies, of all these crimes—the unreasoning childishness of them. For the great part of them were attempted under circumstances which should have shown to even the most dull-witted that there was no chance of success.

It was a wave of strange and terrible crime, indeed, that was sweeping over all the earth. The newspapers concerned themselves with it to the exclusion of all else soon. They sought for explanations. What had caused this sudden release of the most brutal passions of numberless people? Many were the answers. An eminent scientist declared that the nerve-racking strain of modern civilization had reached such a pitch that the human mind could no longer stand it, was giving way beneath it. Many wrote serious letters to the press denouncing the motion pictures as schools of crime. Others defended them. And while the cause was thus argued, the great wave of crime and utter lawlessness that had rolled across earth seemed increasing in volume.

The number of deaths by violence that were each day recorded had grown now to an appalling figure. Murderous attacks were common in every one of earth's great cities. Men hurled themselves at each other's throats, apparently for a word, a gesture. Nor was this all. A strange erratic insanity seemed seizing more and more of earth's millions. Numberless were those reported to the authorities as missing, those who had wandered causelessly away from home and family. The world's roads held an unprecedented number of vagrant wanderers.

But in a few days more even this astounding wave of appalling crime was dwarfed in importance by more astounding and more terrible happenings. Accidents, a great number of them fatal to many, were occurring in every part of earth in an amount that was all but incredible.

More than a hundred people had gone to death in the crash of two thundering passenger trains in Colorado, a crash that had been due to the failure of an engineer to heed the plainest of signals. Two train wrecks in northern England had taken a toll of life almost as great, and there were reports of many other crashes from various parts of earth. In every one the accident had been due to the inexplicable failure of the human element, the failure of dispatcher or switchman or engineer to perform the duty that habit should have made automatic. In one case, that of the Austrian disaster, the crash had been directly caused by the sudden craziness of a switchman, who, for some slight grievance, had sent a long passenger-train crashing through an open switch and down an embankment.

There was news as terrible from the seas. Wireless reports flashed thick with word of ships that had blundered fatally on rocks or shoals by fault of helmsman or navigating officer. The greater part of these, fortunately, were freight-ships of medium and small size, but one case sent a thrill of horror through earth, already steeped in horror. That was when the great transatlantic liner Garonia, bound to Southampton, crashed by night into the southern Irish coast with the resulting loss of three-fourths of the thousand humans it carried. And that wreck, like the others, was due to an utterly inexplicable failure of the ship's personnel.

Smaller in magnitude, but taking a total of far more lives, were the unnumbered accidents that took place in the thickly populated and highly mechanized countries of North America and Europe. The number of automobile deaths, always staggering America, reached a stunning total in those last fateful days of September. Crashes took place at every corner, and the running down of pedestrians became a common occurrence everywhere. Many cars mowed a path of death through street and sidewalk before they were halted, their drivers losing apparently all faculty of control of them.

And in mill and shop and factory death's grim hand was reaping as thickly. Men, upon whom the lives of many depended, suddenly lost control of their machines and sent those many to death. Countless others were mangled or crushed to death by the great mechanisms they had operated for years without mishaps. Airplane crashes became so numerous that many sections of the world peremptorily forbade all further flying until the cause of it all could be ascertained. It was as though more and more of the masses of men were becoming incapable of handling the mechanisms, of conducting the operations, that they had been executing for years. Was mankind going collectively insane?

It seemed insanity, indeed, that was sweeping earth now. Riots had taken place on a small scale here and there in those days, but it was not until after the first of October that the first of the great outbreaks took place in London. Crowds of wandering men and women began the looting of shops, the breaking of windows, and the rioting swiftly spread. So swiftly did it spread, in fact, that by the time the troops called to suppress it appeared on the scene, unestimated thousands were engaged in the wild search for plunder. At the order to fire, an irregular volley from the troops killed scores, but in the pitched mob battle that followed scores of the soldiers took the side of the looters. The combat between mob and soldiers was forgotten, and the battle became a wild scene of brutality and violence in which hundreds were slain and trampled. In the end it required machine-guns to disperse them.

A similar great outbreak in New York was curbed quickly a day later by the use of planes and tear-bombs, but two days after there came a huge riot of unexampled bloodiness in Chicago, which cost several thousand lives and which resulted in the burning of a third of the city. Beginning as a race riot and developing into a savage general battle for loot, it was notable for the fact that the troops, called to suppress it, broke up even before they reached the scene and occupied themselves in brutal looting and battle of their own. And a score of great riots in the other cities of earth had similar results.

Civilization seemed crashing, with this oncoming dissolution of its organization and institutions. Had humanity gone insane, indeed? Swiftly, with full realization of the peril upon it by then, a conference of the world's most noted scientists had been called some days before at New York, to explain and to halt, if possible, this wave of seeming insanity that was gripping more of the masses of humanity each day and that was disintegrating civilization.

But when those scientists met, the world learned that they had a hundred different explanations of the thing, no two agreeing. The famous American alienist who had voiced his opinion days before reiterated his belief that the minds of men were giving way en masse beneath the strain of modern civilization. A Rumanian bacteriologist claimed that the thing was the result of a contagious new brain disease spreading over earth, and claimed even to have isolated the bacterium of that disease. The scientists, gripped seemingly by something of the erratic condition of mind they were striving to explain, argued these theories and others with utmost passion, sometimes attacking each other. An English physicist, who suggested that earth was passing through strange mind-affecting gases in space, was assaulted by the proponent of another theory. And still more furious and incredulous, the world learned, was the reception given to the explanation of a New York biologist named Ferson, who claimed that the whole great terror was the result of the human races slipping backward on the road of evolution!

"World atavism! A throwback of all the world's life on the road of evolution!" So, they learned, Ferson had cried to the assembled scientists. "All earth's animal life is beginning to slip back, and man, as the most recently developed animal, is slipping first, is going back toward the savage state, toward the cave-man or troglodyte, toward the ape! He is losing control of his passions as he goes back, which accounts for the violence that now fills earth! And he is losing the mental capacity of modern man, which accounts for his inability to operate longer our modern machines! A world atavism that is beginning with the atavism of the human races!"

"But what could cause such world atavism as that?" the incredulous scientists had cried.

"The evolutionary theory of my former associate, Dr. Grant——" Ferson had begun, but was interrupted by a chorus of derisive shouts provoked by the mention of the scientist whose ridiculous theory had been exploded.

So Ferson had been forced from the meeting by the furious scientists, who seemed seized indeed with the erratic craziness that was gripping the world. Another day they advanced and argued their theories, theories that grew ever more impossible, more incoherent, and then the meeting dissolved in a general riotous brawl of the arguing scientists. They, in common with the rest of the races of men, seemed incapable longer of calm thought, of cool, unpassioned reasoning. Two were killed, throttled in the brawl that ended the meeting, and the rest scattered. They were not followed or punished, for now the disintegration of humanity's institutions had become such that crime was unheeded.

Men were outrivalling each other in mad action. Those in high places as in low were gripped by the insanity that had apparently seized earth, and from the Cabinets and Congresses of a score of nations came declarations of war against other nations, for the slightest of reasons or for none at all. England, the United States, France, Germany, Italy, Turkey, Japan and China—these and a dozen others issued frenzied and incoherent calls to arms. But they were unheeded! Even war now could not penetrate the unreasoning minds of men. Armies had broken up, all discipline and organization vanishing. A few who tried to keep their soldiers in line found that the men could no longer handle the great guns and instruments of war, found that most of them were incapable of the operation of rifles!

Civilization was crashing with a prolonged roar of falling laws and institutions and customs echoing across the world. The ordinary methods of transportation and production having completely broken down days before, the stream of food into the great cities had abruptly ceased. The brutal throngs that filled those cities subsisted by looting the existing food supplies for a time, but soon these were exhausted and then terrible battles took place between the rioters for food which they had found. Battles they were of hordes of ragged brutes, of savages, who fought with knives or with their bare hands in the streets. Only occasionally was a shot heard, for almost none there was now with sufficient dull glimmer of intelligence to manipulate a gun.

In the shadow of the tall towers of New York, and in the brick and stone acres of London and the boulevards of Paris, thousands and hundreds of thousands of these savages swarmed, the ways choked with corpses of the slain. At night they crouched fearfully in hallways and offices and corridors, the vast cities lying dark and silent beneath the stars. Shapes of prowling animals were being seen in some of them by night. No wheel turned in all the world now, for none seemed left with intelligence enough to operate the simplest machine.

And these swarms that had been human were changing in appearance too. The men were unshaven and hairier, it seemed. Much clothing had been discarded, crude belts that held knives or the like weapons being retained. They crouched now as they walked, their step a watchful, animal-like one. From under shaggy brows they stared at each other. Small, crude family-groups held together, the man battling other men for the possession of food. Some managed to kill animals, and wore the skins.

They were troglodytes, millions of them, men such as the world had seen thousands of years before, as humanity had been then. They were troglodytes, wandering through the cities and towns that they themselves had built, staring in wondering fear about them at things the purpose of which they could not understand. But most had no wonder, only a brutal lack of interest in all save food and mating and sleep. There were no fires, for all had lost the use of fire and feared it now.

Driven by hunger, great masses of them were pouring out of the cities into the countryside, to hunt roots and herbs and to kill small animals for food. They made rude shelters for a time, then abandoned them for caves and crannies in the rocks. They ceased to use knives or spears, they could but throw great stones at each other or wield chance clubs, or fight with bare hands.

Many had remained in the cities and among them was more fighting. With each day they were changing farther, it seemed, going farther back along the long road of change that man had ascended so slowly through the ages, and that he was slipping back upon so swiftly.

The streets of New York and Glasgow and Constantinople and Yokohama saw them, these animal-like, ape-like hordes that wandered there. Ape-like they were becoming, indeed, swiftly hairier of body, more crouching of gait, stooping occasionally in moving to run on hands and feet. Clothing they had discarded. The fragmentary, mumbled speech that they had kept until days before had given way to a meaningless medley of barking shouts and cries whose tone conveyed their crude attempt at communication. They roamed the great cities in little groups or tribes, of each of which one was the strongest, the tyrant, the acknowledged lord.

And now, they were changing still. Were running more on hands and feet, walking upright less. Back from man to troglodyte, and from troglodyte to ape had the human races gone, and now were slipping back still into the animal races from which the apes had come! World atavism—and it was wiping the last human-like forms from the face of earth!

***

Of this great change that in days swept man back into the brutal forms of dead ages, I, Allan Harker, was a witness from the first. For it was at New York that the early manifestations of the change had been first noticed, in that increasing wave of terrible crime that was in days to rage over the whole earth.

Neither Ferson nor I, of course, had any suspicion of the thing's real magnitude in those first days. We followed, with the same astonishment that held most in the world, the astounding growth of crime and violence, but it was remote from our own interests, and we were both very much absorbed in our differing work of experimentation. We spent more time on that work, indeed, in those days than before, for both Ferson and I seemed to have lost a little of our usual skill and knowledge. I know that he caught himself in inexplicable lapses, and I know that I, usually the most patient of biologists, forgot myself in sudden impatient rage on one or two occasions and smashed retorts and test-tubes about me. Neither of us dreamed, of course, that we were being affected by the same strange forces that were releasing humanity's passions in a carnival of crime.

But when a little later the great wave of crime that was making earth hideous was made more terrible by the innumerable inexplicable accidents that were occurring, Ferson became thoughtful. He deserted his own white-tiled laboratories for the university's psychological test-rooms with their strange recording instruments, and spent hours there carrying out intricate tests of the reactions of himself and others. It was after two days of such tests, when the fatal accidents occurring everywhere were taking toll of thousands of lives daily, and when almost all industrial activity was slowing and stopping because of them, that Ferson came back, his countenance as I had never seen it.

"I've found it, Allan," he said quietly. "The cause of all this terror—these innumerable crimes and accidents and riotings."

"The cause of them?" I repeated, uncomprehendingly, and he nodded.

"Yes, and that cause is world atavism! An atavism, a throwback, of all the world's animal life, that is beginning with man as the most recently developed animal and that is taking place before our eyes! Taking place in ourselves even!"

"World atavism!" I gasped. "But, Ferson—that such a thing could be—it's inconceivable!"

He shook his head. "Not inconceivable. You remember Grant and his theory, that the evolution vibrations from the sun were what had pushed earth's life up the road of evolution? And you remember that Grant said that were those evolution vibrations to cease to reach earth from the sun, all earth's life would slip swiftly back upon that road?"

"I remember," I said, "but how could such a thing happen? What could ever halt the play of the sun's evolution vibrations on earth?"

Ferson's eyes were somber. "I do not know what could," he said slowly, "but I think I know who could!"

"Ferson!" I cried. "You don't for an instant think that Grant——"

"I do think so," he said, his voice steelly. "Grant discovered the existence of the evolution vibrations—he alone of men knew all concerning them. Do you remember what he said when they refused to let him explain his theory even at that meeting? He said: 'I will give you proof of this. I will give you proof yet of this theory, and such a proof as the world has never seen before!'"

My mind was reeling. "Then you think that when Grant disappeared—that he——"

"I think that that great proof that Grant promised in his rage to give the world is the world atavism that is upon humanity now! I think that Grant in some inconceivable way has used his knowledge and his power to deflect or dampen the evolution vibrations coming toward earth from the sun, and that it is because of the absence of those vibrations that earth's life is slipping backward!"

"But where will it stop?" I exclaimed.

"It will not stop, Harker—this tremendous change has only begun. Man, the most recently evolved of all animals, is changing first, and will go back through troglodyte and ape to the forms before them, back through changing beast-forms. By then the other animals of earth will be changing also, thrown back along the evolutionary road, and that great atavism will continue until earth's life has all changed back into the first crude protoplasmic forms from which eons ago it sprung!"

"But what can we do?" I cried. "There must be some way of stopping this!"

"There is only one way," he said. "Grant is causing this great world atavism, is shutting off the sun's evolution vibrations from earth by projecting toward the sun, no doubt, a great dampening or neutralizing vibration that stifles them, annihilates them, at their source. We must find Grant's whereabouts, must destroy whatever apparatus he is using to do that!"

"Yet if all are changing—we two also must be changing!" I exclaimed, and he nodded.

"We two are already a little affected as all men are, more or less. Our lapses of memory, the difficulties we have in our work now, these things in the last days are the result of this world atavism in us, just as the crimes and accidents filling earth are. And we two must protect ourselves against this tremendous change, whatever we do, for on us depends the one chance of halting Grant's terrible work. The world will never believe that that dread work is really going on until it is too late, so you and I must not change!"

Ferson went swiftly on to explain his idea. This was none other than to construct two small projectors that would each automatically and ceaselessly generate artificial evolution vibrations, vibrations affecting a limited range as the sun's vibrations had affected all earth. These projectors in their compact cases could be worn on our bodies by each of us without being noticeable, and would keep each of us always thus in the range of the vital vibrations, so that we would not be affected by the world-wide absence of that which was causing this world atavism. Whatever great dampening wave Grant was sending out toward the sun to neutralize its evolution vibrations would not, of course, affect the vibrations of our own little projectors.

The next two days saw us at work upon these projectors. The method of producing the evolution vibrations we knew, for as I have mentioned, they had been artificially produced in a small way by physicists upon Grant's first announcement of his theory. The second day, therefore, saw our projectors complete, small flat black cases that were strapped to our belts without being noticeable, each holding the tiny but marvelously powerful batteries that were the current-source, and the compact little generator that automatically and unendingly released the vital evolution vibrations for a range of several feet. With these completed and working, and secured thus by them from being ourselves affected by the terrible atavism that was upon the races of man, we began our greater work of locating Grant and the apparatus by which he was shutting off the sun's vibrations and loosing this horror on the earth.

For horror it had now become, and the world was waking up to its true nature as every sort of brutal passion was released in terrible crime over it, and as the inexplicable mindlessness of men brought on terrific accidents. Already a dozen of the greatest governments in coöperation had called a conference of earth's greatest scientists at New

York to explain or to halt at least the horror that was sweeping earth. To that conference they came with each a different and more incredible explanation of the thing, and to it went Ferson and I to give them the true explanation and to turn them toward the search for Grant that might yet save humanity. But that explanation was never given, for Ferson's first mention of world atavism was greeted with incredulous cries, and when he went on to mention Grant, such a derisive storm arose, that he was forced bodily from the meeting, leaving the scientists disputing fiercely over the most impossible of theories, supporting and opposing those theories by blows.

For they, like the rest of humanity, seemed incapable now of clear and sustained thought upon any subject. Even Ferson and I, working day and night in the isolated upper Manhattan laboratories of the university, were able to see clearly what was happening about us. We were living, eating, sleeping at the laboratories by this time, for all means of transportation and all industrial activities were ceasing. Great masses of men roamed the streets of the city, some forming into gangs that made life terrible for the others, the rest engaged in indiscriminate looting. The great London riot and the abortive outbreak in lower New York had now taken place, and it was evident to all that the last shadow of law and order in the city was vanishing, for more and more the troops and police who maintained it were engaging in the rioting themselves.

News came still a little, in incoherently written and erratically printed sheets, for a few days, and it was thus we learned of the huge Chicago riot and subsequent fire. It marked the beginning of the end. Within a few days more utter lawlessness reigned over New York, corpses lay in its streets and looters were everywhere. The university buildings, deserted now by all but ourselves, were not attacked except on a few occasions by the looting swarms, there being no food or other desirable things in them, and Ferson and I had rifles and pistols in our laboratory to repel the ragged and brutal gangs that might attack us.

In those terrible days we were occupied heart and soul in the work of locating Grant and whatever mechanism it was by which he was casting this doom on humanity. It was Ferson's idea that the great damping wave, which Grant must be sending toward the sun to halt the play of its endless evolution vibrations, would affect certain recording instruments, if the correct frequency for their circuits could be found. Once that was found, by observing the amount by which the instruments were affected at different locations by the waves of the great damping vibration, we could calculate and chart that great wave's source with some degree of accuracy. It seemed to me a very slender chance, yet I knew as well as did Ferson that it was the one possible way. Grant, we knew, would have protected himself, as we had, by a small artificial projector of the vibrations.

So in those fearful days we worked with the recording instruments, watching them at each new trial for some indication of the force whose source we sought. The whole great mass of New York's giant structures that stretched southward and downward from our laboratory lay now in complete darkness each night; the last wonted activities of civilization having ceased in it as elsewhere. Ragged hordes of savages roamed it, savages so hairy and crouching and brutal of face, seeming each day more prognathous of jaw and slanting of brow and animal-like of eye, that we knew them to be troglodytes, cave-men, men such as humanity had been ages before and such as it was over all earth now.

We saw them occasionally prowling through the university grounds in search of food, shambling toward us with lowering brows to attack us when they glimpsed us, but fleeing in fear when we fired over their heads. For none of them could manipulate so complicated a thing as a firearm. All earth's hundreds of millions were prowling their way in just such brutal bands, thrown back to the state that had been man's before history's dawn. And ever more brutal and hairy and animal-like they were becoming as they slipped back farther still, back from troglodyte to ape! Mankind was gone, transformed into these still-changing brutes—all except Ferson and me.

***

I cannot tell now in full of those terrible last days of change, those days in which in our chance glimpses we saw men making that other terrible step backward, from troglodyte to ape. For Ferson and I were working with the speed of utter despair. Even were Grant's terrible work to be halted, the sun's evolution vibrations again released on earth, it would take them untold ages to raise the brute-like beings about us to the status of men once more. Humanity was passing, had passed, into the brute around us, yet for their sake, for the sake of the humanity that might rise again in the dim future, we kept to our efforts, sought still to halt this awful change, that would otherwise not stop until protoplasmic slime alone was left living on earth.

We had found the correct frequency for the circuits of our recording instruments, and in feverish haste set up those instruments at intervals of a mile, working through the night. The weirdest of work it was, the vast city's streets and structures silent in the night around us, the countless hordes of brute-like beings that once had built them now cowering in the buildings in ape-like fear of the night's mysteries. We took our readings, hastened back to our laboratory, and dawn found us marking those readings on the great chart-map of the section we had ready. Somewhere in that section, somewhere near New York, we knew, Grant lurked with his terrible mechanism, our first readings having shown us that. And now, as with trembling hands Ferson and I drew the graphs on the big chart, we stared for a moment after in complete silence.

Those lines converged at a point in a midtown block of the great city south of us, a block occupied by a single gigantic building whose aspiring tower was in sight of our laboratory's windows!

For moments Ferson and I stared from chart to tower in silence, and then without words we had turned, seen to the filled magazines of the pistols at our belts, and were passing out of the laboratory into the bright sunlight. As silent as ever, we started southward.

Never, were my existence extended a thousand years, could there be blotted from my memory that journey southward through the silent towers of New York that Ferson and I made then. For the great city that lay silent about us beneath the brilliant noon sunshine, was a city of horror unutterable. Dead lay thick in its streets and great dogs, already strange and fierce and wolf-like, ran in packs among them. The rusting wrecks of smashed automobiles were piled at every corner. No window of all we passed remained intact, sidewalks and streets were sprinkled with shivered glass. Westward across the river a great fire was burning in the cities there, pouring a black volume of flame-laced smoke up to the skies. But more terrible than all of these things were the hordes, the swarms of creatures that moved through the streets and ways about us, the countless creatures that once had been the city's people!

Great ape-like creatures they were, not apes such as men had known, but ape-like races such as men had sprung from eons before. In groups and packs of scores they roamed the city's ways. Covered with thick hair, stooped and crouching of gait, the garments that they had worn as men torn and discarded, there was in them no semblance to humanity. They walked stiffly toward each other, stooping to rest hairy forearms on the ground each few steps. They growled and barked in rage, or chattered volubly and meaninglessly. The majority were prowling in wrecked stores for fragments of food. Others moved along the streets in a search for small animals, for insects even.

Growling in rage their groups came toward Ferson and me as we moved onward, but each time a pistol-shot sent them fleeing from us. We moved on, never speaking, Ferson's face icy calm, my own brain reeling. We came at last to the base of the giant building that we knew must hold whatever mechanism Grant was using to withhold the evolution vibrations from the earth.

Ferson turned to speak to me for the first time. "Somewhere in here," he whispered. "We must search, Harker——to find Grant's apparatus——"

"And if he is with it?" I asked, but his only answer was to tighten his grip on the pistol in his hand.

We passed into the great building's marble entrance hall, a place of dim shadows, through which we stumbled over prostrate dead. We went quickly through the looted, wrecked rooms that had been the luxurious shops of its first level. Then the stairs, and we were going upward, level after level, searching through the immense building's numberless offices and rooms. In one or two were dead, and some had been wrecked, but in none, in no part of the building, it seemed, were any of the ape-like throngs. That seemed encouraging, somehow, and with beating hearts we pressed on upward.

Level after level. We were high in the immense building; its floors here were smaller of extent because of its pyramidal form. Yet there was no sound from the shadows about us, no sign of what we sought. Despair was growing in us, for we were high in the great tower that was the building's uppermost part, and had found nothing. Through the shadowy halls we pressed still, and through the silent rooms lit with the gold of the westward-swinging sun. But as we moved up the narrow stair toward the last and highest level of the great tower, something flamed in Ferson's eyes as in mine.

A sound had come from above to our ears, a steady, slow clicking as of a great clock. Pistols in hand, we moved up, found ourselves in a small hall at the tower's side. The unused elevator-shaft was beside us, and the stairs that led to the roof. But before us was the single door that gave access, apparently, to the whole space of the tower's uppermost level. And from behind it came the slow clicking to our ears!

As one we crossed the hall toward that door. Ferson's hand on its knob turned slowly, and slowly, astoundingly, the door swung open. Our pistols lowered for the moment in our amazement, we stepped through, stopped. A dozen feet before us stood Grant, a heavy automatic in his hand trained upon us.

Silence. In it Grant's eyes held ours. His dark-browed powerful face was lit with unholy triumph, with sardonic exultation. I saw that before us was the whole space of the tower's highest level, thrown into one great room. Huge black-cased and powerful batteries were ranged upon each other in scores at one side of the room. Armored cables led from them through incalculable generators and transformers to a great object at the big room's center. It was like a giant searchlight, a dozen feet or more in diameter, swung in a frame resembling gimbals, so that it could be turned in any direction. The twelve-foot disk inside it glowed silently with white light, and the great thing was turned to face exactly the sinking sun westward. It was slowly following the descending sun, turning slowly under the action of a great clock-mechanism, whose clicking was loud in our ears still.

Grant, Ferson and I——we were silent there in the room, all motionless, until Grant spoke. His voice was metallic, controlled, mocking.

"Ferson and Harker," he was saying. "Ferson and Harker, who believed in my theory, my power, it seems, when none else on earth did. Who made projectors like the one that I wear, and have escaped the world doom that I have released. Have escaped and have come in search of me, with pistols in their hands, even!"

My brain was racing. I knew that to lift the arms in our grasp meant instant death. Grant's sardonic mirth lashed suddenly out in scorn.

"To come through the city toward this building firing shots!" he mocked. "Shots that made those brute-swarms beneath us flee, but that warned me at the same time of your coming! To steal clumsily in upon me that way, thinking to surprise me and halt the work that's not yet finished!"

"That work has gone on too long, Grant," said Ferson slowly, his voice strange. "It cannot go on longer."

"Cannot?" came the bitter voice. "You mistake, Ferson—it must and shall. What are they now but brutes, animals; the world of men that derided and refused my work, that might have transformed them into gods? Brutes, and even more brutal shall they become, going down through form after form to the first protoplasm. They asked for proof——I have given the world proof, have thrown back humanity eons on the road of progress! And I will throw them and all earth's life back farther still! This great projector—— it is worth the months it took to build it—months that I toiled here and posed as a scientist studying electrical phenomena, working to finish the projector at last and turn its great damping vibration toward the sun in a mighty ray! A vibration tuned to neutralize and destroy that part of the sun's evolution vibrations radiating toward earth! You have lost, Ferson——Harker, for you both die this moment and this projector shall continue to withhold the evolution vibrations from earth until its life has been thrown back in this world atavism into the primal protoplasm! Until I alone am left living upon——"

His pistol roared, for it was at that instant that Ferson leaped. But even the bullet could not halt Ferson's rush, so swift and unexpected was it, and he struck Grant, knocked him back, I leaped toward the projector.

Grant's pistol was detonating even as he was knocked back, though, and half-way to the machine something seemed to strike me two swift, smashing blows beneath the shoulder. I swayed, staggered on to the projector, was beneath it and reaching toward the cables leading into it. Grant was springing toward me, his pistol at my head. But behind him Ferson, blood on his lips and on his breast, half-raised himself, the pistol in his hand speaking. At its crack Grant swayed, collapsed and fell, the black compact case at his belt, that had preserved him, breaking loose as he struck the floor.

Ferson, leaning, had his dimming eyes upon me, striving to speak. I reached, grasped the cables, tore at them once, twice, and then they had ripped loose. The white light of the disk inside the great projector vanished, and the mechanism that moved it ceased its clicking. The world atavism, that had thrown the races of man back to the state that had been theirs eons before, was ended at last! Ferson, his eyes on mine, seemed to smile feebly in approval. Then his body slipped quietly down and he lay as motionless and silent as Grant.

Afterword

I have been writing here in this silent room for a time, whose length I cannot guess. Westward, though, the sun is touching the horizon, its level rays searching through this room, over the great projector and over Ferson and Grant, lying silent before me.

My life is ebbing swiftly from me with each passing minute, yet with the age-old instinct of man strong in me I have striven thus to leave a record of the great change, that men of the future in some far day may read.

Men of the future! For there will be such, there must be such. The upward surge of evolutionary progress that has been interrupted, set back, here on earth begins again its slow upward climb with the halting of this projector, the coming again of the evolution vibrations that are now playing on earth again. Beneath me, in the silent city, there swarm the ape-like hordes that were once humanity, but through the coming ages they will climb up again through troglodyte and savage barbarian to man!

And it is for those men of the far future that I have

written with my last strength these words, as a record and a warning that I shall enclose in the steel box beside me.

A warning that their civilization be never cast back from man to brute as ours has been. And if God send that they heed that warning, none among them ever shall die as I die now, the last man of all men, looking down through the sunset into the familiar but infinitely strange city, where roam the hordes that once were men. Sunset! Sunset for our civilization, our races, as for the earth. But, dying, I know that after their passing there must come with the slow upward climb of evolution new races, new civilizations, as surely as after sunset and night must come the——

The End